With Love —
From. Wendy

Christmas 1988

REMEMBER

YOUR

ESSENCE

ALSO BY PAUL WILLIAMS

Outlaw Blues
Das Energi
Coming
Dylan—What Happened?
The Book of Houses (with Robert Cole)
The International Bill of Human Rights (editor)
Waking Up Together
Only Apparently Real: Conversations with Philip K. Dick

PAUL WILLIAMS

REMEMBER YOUR ESSENCE

 HARMONY BOOKS, NEW YORK

for Donna

Published by Harmony Books, a division of Crown
Publishers, Inc., 225 Park Avenue South, New York,
New York 10003 and represented in Canada by the
Canadian MANDA Group
HARMONY and colophon are trademarks of Crown
Publishers, Inc.
Manufactured in the United States of America

Library of Congress Cataloging-in-Publication Data
Williams, Paul, 1948–
Remember your essence.
1. Spiritual life—Meditations. I. Title.
BL624.W57   1987   158′ .1   86–14681

ISBN 0-517-56524-2
10 9 8 7 6 5 4 3 2 1

First Edition

ONE

Picture a burning log, like in a fireplace, a hearth.

Now see it as if it were floating in the air a few feet
in front of you, and notice that there are two elements
here: the log, and the fire that clings to it.

Now move this image of a burning object into your body,
so that you can feel it like a warm, comforting glow
inside your chest.

This burning log is real, and it exists inside you.

The inexhaustible log is called your essence;
and the fire, the flame, is your life.

You are a source of warmth and light.

Children who are cold or lonely or unsure come to you
for comfort, and you always have comfort to give.

Even at your moments of greatest doubt, when you feel
totally closed down to the world and to yourself,
the life still burns in you, and your essence remains
pure and powerful and untouched.

Your fears and resentments may blind you, may
cripple you, may seem to totally absorb you,
but they cannot stop you from being a source of warmth
and light.

You are who you are regardless of who you think you are.

Your thoughts affect your actions, and they affect your perception, your experience, of everything around you.

Your thoughts control your experience of reality.

But your thoughts cannot affect or change or control or even touch who you are.

You have a power that has nothing to do with what you do
or what you say
or who you know or what you know
or where you are or what you look like or your skills
or your talents
or what you have.

It is the power of your presence.

It is the heat and light from your burning log.

And it touches everyone who comes in contact with you.

Your everyday life is like a dream.

Everything that happens in a dream seems very real and very important while it is happening.

And then when you wake up, you say, "Oh! It was only a dream!", and what had been very important becomes "interesting," or maybe you forget it altogether.

You know that it wasn't real in the ways that your everyday life is real.

Everyday life, however, is no more real than a dream is real.

When you wake up, you remember this.

And each time you wake up, you remember again.

Remember your essence.

Forget everything else that you know,
and get back in touch with the feeling
of being who you are.

Remember means re-experience.

Your essence is always there to be re-experienced.

It is an inexhaustible source of nourishment
and support.

It is your most trustworthy and dependable friend.

When you need somebody to lean on,
lean on your experience of who you really are.

Remember that your essence is experienced by you
as a feeling.

The trap is this: wanting to know who you are,
which means you want to be able to say some words,
think a thought, cling to a description.

The question comes: how can I find out what my essence is?

There's nothing to find out.

Remember it. Experience it. Feel the feeling of it.

Let go of your thoughts, let the talk inside your head
drift away, be still and remember who you are.

Breathe slowly, and feel yourself fanning the flame
of your burning log
with every breath.

Now you know.

Now you know, and however many times you forget,
you can always remember again.

(You are required to forget; it's like breathing out,
it makes space for breathing in again.)

Now you know that there is more to you than information.

Now you know that there is more to you than can ever
be expressed by your mind.

You are a secret that cannot be told.

There is no way anyone can know the secret except by
being close to you.

Now you know why people want to be close to each other.

In the cold and the darkness of this universe,
we are attracted by the heat and light of other essences
and the life energy
with which they burn.

Picture yourself holding hands
with five other people in a circle
your eyes are closed
and you become aware
of the burning log inside each person

Six logs in a circle

Now see and feel the light
that all of you give off together.

You are a circle of light.

The purpose of your light
is to enclose a space.

Within this space
life is created.

When you start to distinguish
each individual person's light
from the light that is all of us together,
you are performing a holy act:
you are creating the world.

This is your world.

You have created every aspect, every detail of it
for your own entertainment and satisfaction.

The parts you don't like you created so there would be
parts you don't like.

The parts you don't know about you created because
it wouldn't be any fun if there weren't parts you didn't
know about.

The things you want and don't have you created so
you'd have something to strive for.

The things you'd do anything to have be different
you created in order to provide yourself with motivation.

You created all of it—not by making it but by noticing it,
distinguishing it, separating it out.

Until you came along, it was undifferentiated light.

You turned it into a world of detail, a planet filled
with distinction and life.

You have it exactly the way you want it.

Awesome, isn't it?

Your world reflects your essence.

If you want to see your essence,
drop all your preconceptions for a moment,
and look around.

Notice how it feels.

The most difficult part of creating
is not judging yourself too hard.

When you pass judgment on your essence,
who is doing the judging?

The answer is, some part of you that is not
your essence: your opinions, your thoughts,
your habits, your fears.

These inessential parts of you look at that which
is truly you and say, we're not satisfied, it
isn't good enough.

It *is* good enough.

Your essence is doing its job, which is to be the fuel
that is always there, feeding and supporting the fire that
is your life.

You can depend on your essence. It is always there for you,
and it is always perfect, no matter what judgments and ideas
may flit through your mind about it.

Trust your essence. I know it's not enough to be told to
let go. You need something to support you, something to let go
to. That's what your essence is for.

The most efficient course is to depend on your essence.

There is nothing you need to know.

As of this moment, you are free of any obligations.

You may go in any direction you like.

You are reborn.

You are naked, unprotected, and unfettered.

And you are a source of warmth and light.

The more freedom you give yourself,
the more effective your actions will be.

This is difficult to believe.

Your judgments tell you just the opposite.

You cannot silence your judging self.

What you can do is choose not to listen to it,
not to be run by it.

This is the path of freedom.

Freedom sometimes feels like loss.

Feel it

accept it

let it go.

Loss is part of our daily lives.

Be healed, be healthy, be whole.

When you are feeling loss, the part that you lost
is with you
and you are whole.

The part that you lost is with you.

What if you really believed this?

How different your life would be!

You resist wholeness like you resist death,
because both suggest completion.

You don't really want to believe
that the friend you lost,
the home you lost,
the love you lost
are still with you.

And yet every time you let go of your fear
there you are again

believing

knowing

experiencing freedom.

The God you lost
and the paradise you lost
are also still with you.

And the innocence you lost
sticks out all over.

You are complete.

You are whole.

And you express your wholeness in health, in joy,
in friendship, in devotion, in art, in caring,
in participating, in responding, in sharing,
in loving.

Expressing your wholeness
is expressing your essence.

Picture a burning log
radiating energy
in all the forms of expression
available to you
in your life.

That is who you are.

And your energy is received.
It makes a difference.

This is not something that may come to pass.

This is happening now.

You are expressing your essence now.

All that you have ever been and will ever be
can be seen in every movement you make,
in everything you do and don't do,
right now.

This is what it feels like to be naked
before God
and God's creation.

It doesn't take courage to be naked before God.
All of us are, all the time.

It takes courage to be *aware* of your nakedness,
to feel it and to know that what you do matters
and you're really here
and this is it.

Every day the existence of the universe
depends on whether you care enough
to create it.

This can be felt as a burdensome responsibility
or a joyful liberation.

People know who you really are.

You have a presence that cannot be kept secret.
Your essence is visible, naked,
to anyone who cares enough to experience it.
You are a source of warmth and light.
And your purpose here is to be who you already are.

There is nothing else you need to be doing.
This is it.

Close your eyes, and imagine yourself as a hollow space
surrounded by a circle of light.
This is a safe space.
It is home.
Everything that happens to you happens within this space.

Clear your space.

Take a deep breath from, and let it out to, the north.
Now turn around and breathe to the south.
Now the west, and finally the east.

Breathe to the four points, the four directions,
the four gates of your city.

You can turn your whole body, or you can close your
eyes, imagine your space, and turn your attention.

You can take five minutes, or you can do this in a
couple of seconds.

Your technique doesn't matter.
Just know that it's very easy to clear your space;
and then, remember to do it.

When your space is clear
the whole universe functions at its best.

When you have space for love in your life,
love comes into existence.

It never misses an opportunity.

Wanting love
is a technique you use
to protect yourself
from the love that is all around you.

Desiring a thing
is your clever way
of preventing yourself from having it.

You already have it
but you are afraid of it.

So you yearn and wish
as a way of denying
love's presence.

But your denial only affects your awareness.

It does not change what is.

You have what you have regardless of what you think you have.

You can shut your eyes
and your ears
and your nose and tongue and fingertips
and your burning log will go on blazing
as bright as ever.

You cannot control your essence
or the life-force that consumes it.

The most you can do is pretend
that it isn't there.

But it is here.
Surrender.
Remember.
You don't have to pretend any longer.

You are always perfect love
exactly this way that you are.

Now open your eyes.
Look around.
Welcome to this world you've created.

Thank you
for remembering.

T W O

You are a source.

Something emanates from you.

What is it?

Think of this: energy is everywhere
but it only becomes visible
when it attaches itself to something—
like fire to a stick of wood.

What we see as we watch the flames
is the transformation of that stick of wood.
The essence of the wood is released as energy.

The essence of your being is also released as energy.

The name of this energy is life.

Your essence burns throughout your life
and this fire is your aliveness
and the aspects of your aliveness that can be perceived
are words (expressions),
deeds (everything you do),
and beingness (your presence).

What emanates from you
is heat and light.
You are life-giving.
You are God, and of God, and that through which God
speaks,
acts,
and breathes.

You are alive.

You burn.

Your essence was sent to a particular corner of reality,
a unique place in space and time,
and set on fire.

You were born.

And you will burn, not in hell as we were once told,
but right here, joyously if you so choose,
as long as you live.

Your death is always with you.
It is the most attractive part of you.

When people tell you they love your eyes,
or the way you walk,
it is your mortality they're seeing.

Mortal means "human."

Mortal means "subject to death."
It also means "belonging to this world."

The power of your presence
is directly related
to how much you are in your body.

Fear of death,
denial of death,
make you hold back from life.
To live the fullest possible life,
embrace and accept your mortality.

Let your mortal light shine.

You are a source of energy, a source of heat and light.

Whether they know it or not, other people are touched
by the energy you send out
every time you are present in their lives.

They are touched not by anything you send out consciously,
but by your essence, that which is always there,
the particular way that you are.

You are present in people's lives
when you share a room with them,
whenever they see or hear or otherwise sense you.
You are present in people's lives when they read a letter you
     wrote,
or sit in a chair you made,
or walk on a floor you swept.

Every contact, every connection, no matter how small,
has an impact.
And this impact is not impersonal or interchangeable.
The other person is not simply touched.
He or she is touched by you.

Your presence as the contact takes place makes a difference.

You do not have to make an effort to be present.
Your presence is unaffected by any effort
to emphasize it or suppress it.
As long as you breathe, you burn.
And as long as you burn, your heat and light
touch everyone you come in contact with.

Your pain is part of your presence.

Self-awareness is painful.

You probably think it's only painful
because you aren't good enough.

It's true the pain of awareness
is often the pain
of your sense of separation
from where you'd like to be.

But do not struggle to end this separation!

The more you strive,
the more separation you feel.

Peace comes when you accept the pain of self-awareness,
and abandon hope,
and love yourself as you are.

Picture yourself as a log in a fireplace
that cannot help but burn.

Listen to the sound of this burning log.
Listen to what it is saying:

I wish, I could, I didn't, I should
I am   I am   I am   I am   I am.

Who are you?

You are who burns.

You are who people see.

You are who people never see.

You are who lives at this address,
this particular corner of space and time,
moving through space and time
yet always your corner,
your place,
your space inside a circle of light—
location of beingness—
you.

You are you.
That doesn't sound like much, does it?
But to the child who comes to you for comfort,
it's more than enough.

And all your wishes and coulds and didn'ts and shoulds
don't matter.
He is drawn to your   I am.

We are essences.

Essences are "I am"'s.
They are described by what they do;
and what they do is say, "I am."

Living essences are transmitters of heat and light.

Your essence is what is truly you,
what cannot be taken away from you,
what you can never lose or change or destroy
or get rid of.
The irreducible you.

You can change and transform your entire universe.
You cannot change your essence.

Essences sing to each other.
I am sings to I am.
To burn is to sing.
Fire sings in a fireplace.
Fire clings to its fuel, and sings
of the joy of burning.
And any flammable that gets close enough
spontaneously joins the song.

When you feel out of touch with your essence,
do not struggle to reclaim it.

What is yours can never be taken away from you.

Let go of what you're holding on to,
and everything that is really yours
will appear in your life
as if by magic.

Let go of your plans and schemes
and suddenly in the silence
you will hear the voices of your guides.

You may not know the names of these guides
but their voices will sound familiar.

Remember to ask for guidance.
Remember to listen.

Do not worry about what it is you're listening for.
Be still, and let it come.

Imagine a spring-fed stream
flowing from deep underground,
pure fresh water bubbling out to dance in the light for a while.

There is a quiet space inside you.
Picture yourself standing in that quiet space
as though you were standing in a clearing in the woods,
looking down at a stream that is dancing over the rocks.

There is a stream inside you, and it is your source.
It is a stream of energy that nourishes and inspires,
and it bubbles up from a deep place, a sacred place.
This source feeds you always.

Some call this stream, God's love.

You are nourished always by your spiritual source.
This nourishment has many names: guidance,
inspiration, health.
Strength and courage are also gifts that flow
from our inner connection with the divine.

When you make a good decision, you give thanks for guidance.
When you create something worthwhile, you give thanks
for the energy and inspiration.
You give thanks for health, courage, and endurance.
Thank you.
That means, I acknowledge you as the source.

Acknowledge yourself.
Acknowledge yourself as the source that you are.

As God is your source,
so you are a source of God's light on earth,
in this reality, this universe.
You nourish all things that you come in contact with.

You are a fountain of light.

The light that flows from you
has a special flavor all its own.

No one else
can spread your light in the world.

Those of us who drink
from your fountain
depend on you.

You enrich our lives.

You support us and bring life to us
by being yourself
and letting God's energy flow through you.

Your doubts, your judgments of yourself and others,
are also part of your presence.
Even as you let go of your doubts,
they arise again in different forms.
Do not be discouraged by this.
You are a flame that is always burning.
Your doubts and fears are part of your process.
Everything about you is a source of light.

Do not strive to be perfect.

You are a source of warmth and light
exactly as you are.

Be modest.

Let go of your dreams of perfection,
and let us drink from your fountain now.

The essence that you are
has probably been here forever.

It has struggled to perfect itself
over and over again.

And every time, it has had to settle
for being what it is.

You cannot change your essence.

If you throw it in a deep hole,
you will express your essence from the bottom of a deep hole.

When you accept yourself as you are,
you lose your pictures of success.
You gain new reserves of energy.
And you can see how everything in your life
has led directly to this moment.

Awakening is sudden, and exhilarating;
and it is also very very slow.

Picture yourself as a log in a fireplace.
See the fire around your log.
Feel your constancy, your unwavering presence.
The fire flickers and dances, and the log stands firm.

You are substance, materiality, solidity.
Your fire is your purpose; it brings you to life.
You sustain it, and it consumes you.
Your willingness to burn and be consumed
is what makes you a source of warmth and light.

You are here to remember.
Remember means re-experience.

Every breath you take re-creates
this miracle called your body, your life.

Be aware of each breath,
and you will find yourself in the presence
of the living God.

To breathe is to experience life in its fullness
again and again.

And as you breathe, you remember.

Remember your name.

Say your name out loud,
and acknowledge its power.

Names have power to awaken.
All words begin as names.

Breathe, and listen for your name.

Something is calling you.

Something is calling from the quiet space inside
and from the vast universe all around.

Something is calling you to life.

Something is calling forth the stream inside you
and awakening you
to your connection with the source.

You are always connected to the source.
Something is reawakening
your awareness of this connection.

Something is allowing you to remember
that it is the universe
(not the bank, not your job, not the grocery store)
that supplies your every need.

Something is calling you
to take a risk;
to flow more freely;
to burn hotter, and brighter.

Something is calling you.
It has no name, and it is not something
you have seen or experienced before.
And yet it calls from your past
as well as from your future.
It has power.
You can smell it and taste it.
And even as you feel yourself resisting it,
you are responding to the call.

Your resistance is part of your response.

Remembering
washes up against you
like waves on a beach.

It melts away and returns
again and again,
roaring and whispering.

You hide your head in the sand at times,
hoping to forget.

But still the waves return
and wash against you
and you remember.

And now you are awake
in the small of the night
with the silence.

You listen
and the noises start:
the details of the universe.

You create yourself
by creating the world around you,

still too sleepy
to be afraid
of your power.

Take the first step.

The first step is always perfect
as long as you are ready
to take the step that follows it.

Only by taking the first step
can you find the step that follows it.

In this life
we find our way
by following each step with another.

Take a step
and follow it.

If you start to see a path emerging,
ignore it.

Do not follow a path.
Follow your own footprints.
Your path will create itself.

Know that you are on your path
and do not ask for a description of it.

Each moment follows the previous moment
and all your triumphs and failures,
your good luck and bad luck,
have brought you to right here, right now.

Do not question or evaluate this moment.

Enjoy it. Accept it.
It has taken you all your life to get here.
Relax, and trust the self that has brought you this far.

You will receive your next assignment soon;
and you will know it when you receive it.

Wait quietly, and trust your source.

THREE

You have power.

The impact you have
on other people
and on the world around you
is the visible effect of your power.

Consciously or unconsciously,
you are using your power
at every moment.

Here is a technique for accepting your power.

Imagine or pretend that your power is in your stomach.
Take a few breaths, and let your power
come out of your stomach
and expand in a ball in front of you
as though it were a balloon.

Each breath inflates the balloon a little larger;
three or four breaths make it the size of a basketball.

Now put white light around the balloon.

You can do this with your mind—
just imagine light surrounding the space where the ball is.
Or you can move your hands in front of your stomach,
and feel the light coming out of your hands
and covering the balloon.

Take a few more breaths.
Let the balloon get bigger.
Now look to be sure you didn't miss any places—
that it's really surrounded by light.

Now take some breaths and pull your power in again.

Each breath deflates the balloon,
making it smaller,
until you can pat your stomach with your hand
and know your power is back inside.

Try this technique without thinking about it.
Vary it any way you like.
See how it feels to you.

Your power is a manifestation of your essence.

Beauty is a power.

Intelligence is a power.

Compassion is a power.

Detachment, patience, enthusiasm,
receptivity, persistence, doubt, adaptability
are a few of your many powers.

Your greatest power is love.

You are not alone.

You are part of a greater purpose.
It is not necessary to understand this purpose.
It is not possible to understand this purpose.
It is not even possible to understand your part
in this purpose.

What you can do is catch a glimpse of it
from the corner of your eye.

Love is energy and willingness.

Laziness is unwillingness and lack of energy.

Love and laziness are opposite emotions.

When you struggle against laziness
you engage it, you give it your attention,
you keep it around.

A better approach is to accept that
you're feeling what you're feeling.

Quiet your mind,
trust your essence,
and wait patiently for the weather to change.

Fear and impatience,
doubt, desire,
anger and despair
cannot be controlled or destroyed.

What is possible is to notice these feelings.

Noticing is the first and most important step
in disengaging from destructive forces.

Picture two gears meshing
so that one turns the other.

Now move them apart a little bit,
just enough so the teeth don't touch.

This is the image of disengagement.

When you're angry or scared or depressed or confused
allow yourself to feel what you're feeling.

Notice the feeling.

And if you see yourself
doing something
or wanting to do something
that is or might possibly be inappropriate
unloving
or self-destructive
notice that this is probably in reaction
to what you're feeling.

Don't try to control what you're feeling.

Picture the feeling, picture the action,
and move them apart from each other a little bit,
just enough so their teeth don't mesh.

Now you are free to choose.

Clear your space.
Let go of any judgments that you have
about your feelings.
Let go of any preconceptions about what
the "right" choice would be.

If you've gotten this far,
you may not need to make a choice.
You may already know what to do
or what not to do.

Remember that one of your greatest powers
is your ability to ask for guidance.

When you accept your power
you are protecting yourself
from your fear of your power.

Most people wound themselves in some way
whenever they use more power
than they're willing to admit they have.

You may experience this as a crick in the neck,
a pain in the back,
a headache,
or an upset stomach.

Look and see what wounding reoccurs in your life.

That's your body telling you
that you are wounded in your power.

Accepting your power
is like stretching your muscles
before a session of vigorous exercise.

Stretch your power.

Take it out, expand it,
surround it with love,
let it know that you are aware of it
and value it,
and then welcome it back inside you.

This won't make you more powerful.

What it will do is assist you
in feeling more at home
with your power.

Welcome your wounds.

They are manifestations of hidden fears.

Without them, your fears would stay hidden.

Hidden doubts and fears
build walls around you.

When you humbly acknowledge,
allow yourself to be aware of,
your doubts and fears,
the walls come down.

You are open and vulnerable.

You are imperfect.

You are loveable.

Pretending to be open and vulnerable won't cut it.

This isn't a perfume, or a style of clothing.

People know who you are.

Your vulnerability, not your light,
is your most attractive quality.

All people give off light.

Vulnerable people also let light in.

Loveable means ''able to be loved.''

Vulnerable means ''able to be wounded.''

Love hurts.

Even God's love hurts.

It takes courage to be alive.

It takes courage to be aware
of your nakedness
before God
and woman
and man.

Self-doubt is a power.
It is the first step in self-awareness.

Your doubts and fears remind you
of your vulnerability,
help you feel the pain
and joy
of your imperfect aliveness.

They open you for love.

Love is the sharing of essence.

Your weaknesses are also your strengths;
and your strengths are also your weaknesses.

If in fact you could fix everything you don't like about yourself
there'd be nothing left of any value.

Sometimes you build walls.
And sometimes you open yourself for love.

This cannot change.
You will always be the person that you are.

You are loved.

Let in the light.

Your teachers
are everywhere.

Some you will recognize,
and some you will not recognize.
This is how it must be.

Do not try to know everything.

The purpose of accepting your power
is self-acceptance,
self-awareness,
self-love,
not in some abstract world
but in relation to what you do
and what you say
and who you are
in this world
this day
here and now.

You are responsible
for what you say
and what you do
and who you are.

When you feel overcome
by the pain of this awareness,
remember that you are loved.

Love heals.

It hurts, and it also heals.

This is the mystery.

To remember your essence
is to be aware
of your dependence on something
completely outside your control.

You can trust your essence
or not;
you can trust the universe
or not;
but the fact of your dependence
will not change.

When you accept your dependence
on what is
you find your place in the world.

This happens
not once
but over and over again.

Open your heart.

You are in your place of power
right now.

FOUR

You are an essence
in a world of essences.

You burn,
like those around you burn,
with an energy called life.

Life reaches out to life.
Essences sing to each other.

Your fire, your aliveness, is sustained
by your need to touch
and be touched.

You are afraid
of the touch of fire.

And yet you live for it.

You are also afraid
of your own fire

yet you cannot live without it.

You depend on your inner source
and you depend
on the stimulation
of the essences around you.

You are a flame that must be nourished constantly
by your fuel
and the air around you
or you cannot create
heat and light.

Great power
always requires
great dependence.

The danger of pride
is you forget this truth,
and act without regard for your source.

Remember your dependence.

Remember that power alone
is not enough.

You must constantly ask,
"What is right?"

No one but you
can answer this question.

And the answer itself
is always changing.

It shifts and dances like fire.

There is nothing you could want to have
that would mean as much to you
as the experience of giving of yourself
and being received.

You always have something to give.

You always have an essence to share.

Even at your moments of greatest doubt and darkness,
the fire burns in you
and you are a source of heat and light.

The question "What is right?"
humbly asked,
is a daily, hourly meditation
to reconnect you
with your purpose.

Confidence is a power
that comes from the inner knowledge
that you are at one with your purpose.

Self-doubt and self-examination
are the means by which
a powerful person like you
re-creates this inner knowledge
at each new moment.

You are on your path.

Look around.

Notice what you're feeling.

Ask, "What is right?"

Now you are ready to take the next step.

Confusion is a feeling.

The most effective response to confusion
is patience.

Acceptance leads to clarity.

This is always true.

If you do not have clarity,
look and see what you're not accepting.

Resistance is the opposite of acceptance.

Fighting and despising your resistance
will not lead to acceptance.

It will only create more resistance.

Accept your resistance.

Love yourself exactly as you are.

Love your anxiety.

Anxiety is lack of trust.

You cannot force yourself to trust.

When you love and accept your own anxiety
you defy reason
and give yourself room
to trust or not to trust.

Don't just pretend to give yourself room.

To love yourself as you are
you must let go of, disengage from,
all thoughts and feelings
about how you really should be.

Love is unreasonable.

Love is a feeling, and the expression of a feeling.

It flows through you from your source.

Whenever you wish to give or receive love,
remember the feeling
and let it flow through you.

Remember the feeling of dependence.

Life on earth
depends on a ball of fire
called the sun.

Life energy from the sun
crosses millions of miles of space
and brings you light and warmth.

You are a miniature sun.
That which you depend on
is that which you have to give.

Your resistance creates heat.

Your acceptance creates clarity.

Everything about you is a source of warmth and light.

You cannot know
with your mind
when to resist
and when to accept.

All you can do
is give of yourself,
tell the truth,
and trust your essence.

A friend
is someone
whose presence you enjoy.

Friendship does not depend on
what you say or do.
It isn't about
what you know
or what you look like
or what you have.

Friendship
is the experience
of presence with presence.

Essences present themselves to each other.

When the attraction is strong enough,
there is a mingling of essences:
each receives a part of the other.

You cannot change your essence.

And yet, two essences can touch
and never be the same again.

This is the mystery.

Picture yourself in the presence of a friend.

Can you feel that person's essence?

What is it you feel?

I'll tell you a secret.

That person—your friend—the essence you're in the
presence of—is a teacher for you, if you allow it,
who can serve you in any and every area of your life
that's important to you right now. Everything you
need or want to know at this moment in your life, in
every area where you have a need or desire to grow,
is here. What you require and wish for is available
to you and right in front of you, and all you have to
do to get it is be with this person and notice everything
that happens while you're in his or her presence. An
hour can be enough, if you are awake enough. Five
minutes could be enough. The limitation is your
willingness and ability to let it in. This has nothing
to do with what the other person does. Your teacher
is his or her essence. Your opportunity is to let it
act on you.

The only limit to your growth and learning
is your fear of becoming more powerful.

The only limit to your ability to love
is your fear of being powerful,
the fear that you can't handle it,
this feeling that you can't trust yourself.

To the extent that your trust is conditional and
you have expectations, you're right—
you can't trust yourself. You're almost certain
to get in the way of what you think you want.
You're going to screw things up.

But trust isn't conditional.

Trust yourself, and trust God,
with no strings attached.

Be ready to accept what you get,
and the world is yours.

You're here, and you have fuel and air.

What else do you need?

Let it in.

Burn.

Love.

And remember.